The Bride of Christ Is Not the Church

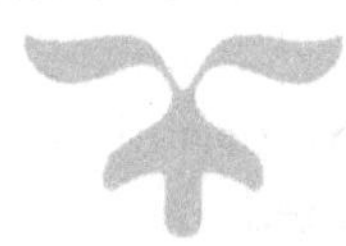

JOHN GEHMAN

ISBN 979-8-89130-407-9 (paperback)
ISBN 979-8-89130-408-6 (digital)

Christian Faith Publishing
832 Park Avenue
Meadville, PA 16335
www.christianfaithpublishing.com

Unless otherwise indicated, the scriptural text presented in this book comes from the New King James Version (NKJV).

Printed in the United States of America

To my joyful Proverbs 31 wife, Joy to my
diligent daughter, Heidi to my fine seven sons:
Answers to my prayer when God responded, "I
will give you some fine young men as sons!"
—His exact words

DISCLAIMER

ALL THE INFORMATION IN THIS book is to be used for informational and educational purposes only. The author will not account in any way for any results that stem from the use of the contents herein. Conscious and creative attempts have been made to ensure that all information provided herein is as accurate and useful as possible. Therefore, the author is not legally bound to be responsible for any damage caused by the accuracy as well as the use/misuse of this information.

CONTENTS

INTRODUCTION

THE WRITING OF THIS BOOK was initiated at the time of the US Senate hearings for the confirmation of a female nominee to the Supreme Court of the United States. This nominee was asked to define the word *woman*. This was at a time in the life of our culture when political correctness had become dominant and human genders had exploded from two to thirty-two and beyond. The nominee confessed that she could not define *woman*.

This admission was disturbing to me and in my mind and in the minds of at least one-half of the country's population; she had just disqualified herself. Even more disturbing was the fact that she was confirmed to be a Justice.

Being a physician, I could not let go of this incident, and also being married to a wonderful woman, a very precious gift from God, I was inspired to write out my definition of *woman*. While my thoughts were coming together on this, I was reminded of Eve, the first woman. She was created to perfection to be the wife of Adam.

Here is my definition of *woman*:

- created last, therefore highest of God's creation
- exquisitely designed for her husband to enjoy
- uniquely designed as a channel whereby the blessing of new human life is brought into this dimension
- uniquely designed to nurture that life
- gifted with wisdom and an uncanny sixth sense enabling her husband in his work
- an essential member of the family

After writing this, I read it and wondered, *Where did this come from?* I give God the glory.

I'm sure you are wondering what qualifications this country doctor has to discuss a theologically controversial subject like the Bride of Christ, especially when his contention is that the church is not the Bride. Have I been to seminary? No, but I have spent much time in Bible study and praying in the spirit whereby I believe I have received insights by which I can provide new information from a physician's perspective. Please be patient as I expound for you.

It is generally assumed by the church at large that the Bride of Christ is synonymous with the church. Nowhere in Scripture does it say that they are the same. With this book, I have attempted to make the distinction.

Also, herein you will find detail that will startle you; however, many new concepts written here are solidly grounded in Scripture. This may not be a new revelation but rather a new interpretation or the uncovering of truth lying dormant in Scripture for two thousand years.

Concerning the discussion on circumcision, certainly, Jewish folks need to understand the prophetic nature of circumcision and how it was fulfilled in Jesus by His crucifixion. For the church, the allegorical description of the person of Jesus is an astonishing revelation and His precious blood takes on new significance. Also there is a new understanding of the Holy Spirit in relation to the Bride.

CHAPTER 1

Types and Shadows

IN THE MID-1980S, I WAS privileged to hear a sermon preached by Wallace Heflin, director of Calvary Campground in Ashland, Virginia. A statement he made seemed to be directed toward me. He stated, "Eve, the wife of Adam, is a type or shadow of the Bride of Christ. The first bride in Scripture is a type of the last bride in Scripture." For those of you, my readers, who don't understand what is meant by types and shadows, let me explain. In the New Testament, in Colossians 2:17 and in Hebrews 8:5 and 10:1, it is pointed out that the Old Testament Law was a shadow of things to be fulfilled in Christ. Several examples that may be more easily understood are as follows:

Deliverance of the children of Israel from slavery in Egypt (Exodus 12) is a type of our salvation from the bondage to sin and the freedom that it provides.

Stand fast therefore in the
liberty by which Christ has made

us free, and do not be entangled
again with a yoke of bondage.
(Galatians 5:1)

The Passover lamb is a type of Jesus. "The Lamb
of God who takes away the sin of the World" (John
1:29). The blood on the door posts and lintel is a
type of the bleeding of Jesus caused by the nails in
His hands and the crown of thorns He endured on
the Cross. Also, Jesus said, "I am the door" (John
10:7 KJV). Each family member to be delivered from
bondage had to walk through that doorway. This was
a personal encounter with the sacrifice of Jesus for
each person, in which with His death, we die to sin.
Jesus, being the Good Shepherd, went on to say, "By
me if any man enters in, he shall be saved and shall
go in and out and find pasture" (John 10:9 KJV).
Passage through the divided waters of the Red Sea
is a type of baptism in which we are buried with
Christ and resurrected to be received into the Body
of Christ. In 1 Corinthians 10:1–2 (KJV) we read,

Moreover, brethren, I would
not that ye should be ignorant,
how that all our fathers were
under the cloud, and all passed
through the sea. And were all
baptized unto Moses in the cloud
and in the sea.

The promised land is a type of the Christian life with its joys and also with trials and tribulations.

Sarah, the wife of Abraham, died and their son, Isaac, was in deep mourning for his mom. Abraham decided that it was time to find a wife for Isaac. He didn't want him to marry any of the local Canaanite girls, so he sent his servant Eliezer back to Haran where they had relatives to find a wife for Isaac (Genesis 24). Eliezer found Rebekah. Rebekah and her family received Eliezer and listened to his story. The choice of Rebekah for Isaac was the answer to Eliezer's prayer. Rebekah agreed to be Isaac's bride. She received the many precious gifts that Eliezer had brought for her, and she returned to Canaan with him.

In this account, Abraham is a type of God the Father; Isaac is a type of the Son, Jesus; Eliezer is a type of the Holy Spirit; Rebekah is a type of the Bride of Christ; the precious gifts are a type of the gifts of the Spirit. Abraham and Isaac were Jews, the first Jews, because of the rite of circumcision. Rebekah was a Gentile, so we see here that she is a type of a Gentile Bride of Christ.

Isaac and Rebekah had a son named Jacob. Jacob also a Jew, when he was grown went to Haran to find a Gentile bride (Genesis 29). He found Rachel and immediately fell in love with her. Jacob worked out a bride-dowry arrangement with Laban, her father, for his younger daughter Rachel's hand in marriage. Jacob would work seven years to receive Rachel as his bride. After seven years, the wedding took place in the late evening. The next morning, Jacob awoke shocked to discover that he had been making love all night with the elder daughter, Leah! Jacob, of course, was furious with Laban for deceiving him, but he received Rachel one week later with the agreement that he would work another seven years for her. Because Jacob loved Rachel more than Leah, Leah despised Rachel. Rachel here is a type of the Bride of Christ.

Rachel gave birth to Joseph our next example (Genesis 37): Joseph had one brother and ten half-brothers. He was the favorite son of his father, Jacob, being his son by Rachel.

At age seventeen, Joseph had dreams in which he was going to be a VIP, and his brothers would one day bow down to him. Unfortunately, he told his dreams to the whole family. This caused his brothers to hate him. The account of Joseph's life in the Old Testament is a type of the life of Jesus in the New Testament. The similarities are as follows:

- Joseph was rejected by his brothers.
- Jesus was rejected by Judas and the Jewish leadership.

- Joseph was sold for the price of a slave, twenty pieces of silver.
- Jesus was sold for the price of a slave, thirty pieces of silver.

- Joseph had victory over temptation.
- Jesus had victory over temptation.

- Joseph provided bread for Egypt.
- Jesus provides *living bread* for the whole world.

Elkanah had two wives (1 Samuel 1). Hannah was his favorite, most beloved wife. Peninnah, the other wife, despised Hannah. The issue was that Peninnah could bear children; Hannah was barren. Hannah cried out to God in her spirit. She promised God that if she could get pregnant and have a son, she would give her son to the Lord's work in the house of the Lord in Shiloh. God honored her prayer. Hannah conceived and gave birth to Samuel, one of the greatest prophets of God in the Old Testament.

Throughout church history, Eve has been despised because of her role in the fall of man, though she is the mother of us all. Leah despised Rachel. Peninnah despised Hannah. The church right now despises the Pentecostals, the Charismatics, and the Full Gospel folks. And so, it goes.

To add insult to injury, the Bride of Christ will be a Spirit-filled young Gentile Bride. The reason for her being Gentile is that Israel rejected her Messiah. She also rejected the teachings of the Apostle Paul, so he turned to the Gentiles who received his teachings gladly. The church is predominantly Gentile. The reason the Bride will be young is that the church is two thousand years old. The modern-day movement of the Holy Spirit started with the Welsh revival in 1904 and continued to Azusa Street in Los Angeles in 1906. People poured in from around the world to witness and experience the Holy Spirit's power. There was such an outpouring of the Holy Spirit, it was unreal.

There were so many astonishing and unbelievable healings and miracles the local media stopped reporting them for fear of losing readership. Therefore, we can say that the Bride of Christ having been birthed in 1904 is a young Spirit-filled Gentile Bride. The outpouring of the Holy Spirit in the church today is expanding exponentially, not so much in America as in Third-World countries.

CHAPTER 2

Image of God

THE BOOK OF GENESIS IS the most incredible book ever written. In the first two chapters, we have the account of how the universe came into being as well as the origin of life, plant life, animal life, and human life. The intelligence and power behind it all, the supreme life, without beginning or ending, is God.

The universe is awesome beyond awesome. No words in any language can begin to describe it. David said it best:

> The heavens declare the glory of God; And the firmament shows His handiwork.
> Day unto day utters speech,
> And night unto night reveals knowledge. There is no speech nor language.
> Where their voice is not heard. (Psalm 19:1–3)

In other words, the glory of God is shouting at us! Are you listening? And look at the order of it all. If that doesn't tell you that God exists, nothing will.

Viewed with the naked eye, viewed through a microscope, an electron microscope, through a telescope, the Hubble telescope, the new James Webb space telescope, you can see what an awesome Creator God is!

The Apollo astronauts looked back from the moon and described Earth as a huge blue marble rotating slowly through space in its path around the sun. They were overwhelmed and glorified God.

> The fool has said in his heart,
> there is no God. (Psalm 14:1)

Our lives were planned by God before the foundation of the world.

> Blessed be the God and
> Father of our Lord Jesus Christ,
> who has blessed us with every
> spiritual blessing in the heavenly
> places in Christ, just as He chose
> us in Him before the foundation
> of the world, that we should be
> holy and without blame before
> Him in love. (Ephesians 1:3–4)

God wanted a family. His purpose in creating the earth was to provide and prepare a place for His family (Psalm 115:16). God is love, and His family planning was loving and only positive, to bring new human life into existence, to multiply and replenish the earth as he instructed our first parents to do and gave them the ability to do just that!

God created man in His own image. The word *image* is used three times in this account. The definition of the word *image* in the Hebrew dictionary is translated as "usually referring to an object of worship."[1]

If man looks like God, then God must look like a man. In Scripture, we see that God has a heart, hands, feet, back parts, and a face. God is referred to with the male pronoun *He*, so the question in many people's minds, which is never asked, "Does God have male genitalia?" Please hold that question for later.

Man was created male and female, but the female was not immediately apparent. When Adam named all of the animals, undoubtedly, he wondered, *Where is there a mate for me?*

> And the Lord God caused a
> deep sleep to fall on Adam, and
> he slept; and He took one of his
> ribs, and closed up the flesh in

---

[1] In my research for this book, I have depended heavily on *Strong's Concordance*, which includes Hebrew and Greek dictionaries. You don't have to know Hebrew or Greek to use the dictionaries. You can also use the Blue Letter Bible online to search this and more.

> its place. Then the rib which the
> Lord God had taken from man
> He made into a woman, and He
> brought her to the man. (Genesis
> 2:21–22)

This woman, retrospectively, had to be the most perfectly gorgeous woman of all time! God gave her to be Adam's bride. Adam said, "She shall be called Woman because she was taken out of Man" (Genesis 2:23). Later he named her Eve (life) "because she was the mother of all living" (Genesis 3:20).

My contention is this: Just as Eve was drawn out of the body of the first Adam, so will the Bride of Christ be drawn out of the body of the last Adam, Jesus Christ, the Body of Christ, which is the church. The first bride in Scripture is a type of the last bride in Scripture.[2]

The church is the Body of Christ as is recorded numerous times with Christ being the Head.

> And He (Jesus) is the head
> of the body, the church: who is
> the beginning, the firstborn from
> the dead; that in all things He
> might have the preeminence.
> (Colossians 1:18)

---

[2] Paul discusses the first man Adam and the last Adam in 1 Corinthians 15:45–49.

> For as we have many mem-
> bers in one body, but all the
> members do not have the same
> function, so we, being many, are
> one body in Christ, and individ-
> ually members of one another.
> (Romans 12:4–5)

> And He (God) put all things
> under His (Jesus) feet, and gave
> Him to be head over all things to
> the church, *which is His body*, the
> fullness of Him who fills all in
> all. (Ephesians 1:22–23, empha-
> sis added)

When God created Adam, Eve was present in the body of Adam but not yet manifested. In the same manner, when God established His church, the Bride was present in the Body of Christ and is yet to be manifested as such.

CHAPTER 3

Mysteries

MYSTERY IS A NEW TESTAMENT word not found at all in the Old Testament. Jesus is recorded using the word three times, each time in His telling of the parable of the sower. The Greek word that is translated as *mystery* is defined as "secret, often refers to a misunderstood part of the Old Testament that with Christ's coming is now unveiled."

The word *parable* is used frequently in both the Old and New Testaments. The Hebrew word is defined as "a wisdom saying, a brief story with a symbolic meaning, a discourse type of prophecy." The Greek word is defined as "an illustration that teaches in a story or extended figure of speech."

The parable of the sower is found in three of the four Gospels. In Mark 4:3–20 (KJV), we read:

> Hearken; Behold, there went out a sower to sow:

> And it came to pass, as he sowed, some fell by the way side, and the fowls of the air came and devoured it up. And some fell on stony ground, where it had not much earth; and immediately it sprang up, because it had no depth of earth: But when the sun was up, it was scorched; and because it had no root, it withered away. And some fell among thorns, and the thorns grew up, and choked it, and it yielded no fruit. And other fell on good ground, and did yield fruit that sprang up and increased; and brought forth, some thirty, and some sixty, and some an hundred. And he said unto them, He that hath ears to hear, let him hear. And when he was alone, they that were about him with the twelve asked of him the parable. And he said unto them, unto you it is given to know the mystery of

the kingdom of God: but unto them that are without, all these things are done in parables: That seeing they may see, and not perceive; and hearing they may hear, and not understand; lest at any time they should be converted, and their sins should be forgiven them. And he said unto them, know ye not this parable? and how then will ye know all parables? The sower soweth the word. And these are they by the wayside, where the word is sown; but when they have heard, satan cometh immediately, and taketh away the word that was sown in their hearts.

And these are they likewise which are sown on stony ground, who, when they have heard the word, immediately receive it with gladness. And have no root in themselves, and so endure but for a time: afterward, when affliction or persecution ariseth for the word's sake, immediately they are offended. And these are they which are sown among thorns, such as hear the word, and the cares of this world, and

> the deceitfulness of riches, and
> the lusts of other things enter-
> ing in, choke the word, and it
> becometh unfruitful. And these
> are they which are sown on good
> ground, such as hear the word,
> and receive it, and bring forth
> fruit, some thirtyfold, some sixty,
> and some an hundred.

The disciples questioned Jesus as to the reason He was teaching in parables. In effect, He said, "Many in the audience do not want to hear the truth and are looking to find fault with what I am saying. Others are trusting folks who understand and believe, therefore the parables."

But Jesus told the disciples, "It is given for you to know the mysteries of the Kingdom of God. If you don't understand this parable without someone explaining it to you, how will you understand any parable?" (Mark 4:11–13 paraphrased). Obviously then, not only are we entitled to know the meaning, but it is incumbent upon us to study the scriptures and decipher the secrets or the mysteries. In fact, *that is what Jesus is challenging us to do.*

Apostle Paul uses the word *mystery* many times, usually in stating that the Gentiles are also to have the Gospel preached to them: "a mystery hidden since the world began" (Romans 16:25b). He mentions also in Colossians 2:2b–3: "the mystery of God, both the Father and of Christ, in whom are hidden all the treasures of wisdom and knowledge."

So Paul, too, is signifying that we are entitled to seek out the solution to mysteries to gain wisdom and knowledge, thereby increasing our understanding of God and His Word.

So how does one receive an understanding of the mysteries? In 1 Corinthians 14:2, it is described in one way, aside from the reading of the Word, to purposefully receive answers:

> For he who speaks in a tongue does not speak to men but to God, for no one understands him; however, *in the spirit he speaks mysteries.* (Emphasis added)

A word of explanation here is in order: There are several aspects to speaking in tongues. One is the prayer language in which one is praying in tongues privately. Another is a message in tongues which is spoken aloud to the congregation by a person with that gift which message is followed by the interpretation either by the same person or another person with the gift of interpretation. I believe this verse is referring to the prayer language in the Spirit which is received upon receiving the baptism of the Holy Spirit. The phrase "he speaks mysteries," I believe, means he speaks *concerning* mysteries or questions that have been in his mind, and God is revealing the answers into his mind or spirit. Much of what I am writing I have received in this biblical New Testament manner.

Prophet Amos wrote in Amos 3:7,

> Surely the Lord God does nothing, unless He reveals His secret to His servants the prophets.

Apostle John wrote in John 15:14–15 quoting Jesus,

> You are My friends if you do whatever I command you. No longer do I call you servants, for a servant does not know what his master is doing; but I have called you friends, for all things that I heard from My Father I have made known to you.

I am not a prophet, only a servant of God. I feel highly honored to receive these insights and am greatly humbled by this experience.

CHAPTER 4

Covenant of God

THIS CHAPTER WAS WRITTEN WITH some fear and trepidation, praying for the Lord's express will. This revelation came to me in the 1980s while I was serving eight months of a three-year sentence in jail for a *crime* that I did not commit. Jail time for me was perfect for studying the Word as I was in the work release area where the other guys were out working various jobs during the day, and I was mostly by myself. I see this now as the hand of God for my benefit. I had almost no distractions. I had previously received the baptism in the Holy Spirit and had done a forty-day fast on V8 juice alone, while reading the Bible from cover to cover aloud.[3] In so doing, I was reading the Word and hearing it simultaneously and realized it was the equivalent of reading it through twice. I had

---

[3] The purpose of the fast was that I was seeking the favor of God because I was facing a trial after two years of adverse publicity. I was convicted and now serving the sentence handed down.

previously read the Bible from beginning to end six or seven times.

When I received this revelation in my spirit, I heard a still small voice or an impression that I would one day be writing this information in a book. I dismissed the idea, not being sure where it was coming from, but I have never forgotten it. While writing this chapter and praying, I continued to have peace about it in my spirit. As you read it, don't be prudish. These are allegorical descriptions.

It is recorded in the Old Testament that after 430 years in Egypt (Exodus 12:40–41), the children of Israel had become idol worshipers like their neighbors, the Egyptians. The golden calf was a god of fertility. Several other gods of that day were gods of fertility with the people beseeching the spirits to provide rich soil, rain, and sunshine for their crops.

Some of these fertility gods were sexual in nature, such as Diana of the Ephesians, who was characterized as having many breasts covering her torso. Also, there was the erect human male organ or phallus. In Deuteronomy 4:16, God warned and commanded the Israelites through Moses not to make any graven image in "the likeness of a male or female." This commandment Israel rejected and suffered the consequences many times over.

As you can imagine, *sacred* prostitution and even orgies were an integral part of worshiping these idols. This angered God greatly. Homosexuals are engaging in this kind of idolatry. Seven times in the

Old Testament, it is recorded that God is a jealous God concerning idol worship.

God called Abram (Genesis 12) out of his idol-worshiping country apparently because he was a believer in a Higher Power. God spoke to Abram and directed him to the land of Canaan with the promise to give him extreme fertility and make of him a great nation, bless him, and make his name great, also that he would be a blessing to all the families of the earth. Abram responded by building an altar and worshiping God. And God blessed Abram, who became very wealthy.

Sarai, Abram's wife, was barren and was way past childbearing years, yet Abram believed in the promise of God concerning their fertility. Years went by, and still no pregnancy.

Finally, Abram called out to God concerning the promise and told God that he did not want to leave his wealth to Eliezer, his steward, an immigrant from Syria. God renewed His promise to Abram, showing him the night sky with the myriad stars, and confirmed that indeed his descendants would be as countless as the stars in number. God changed Abram's name to Abraham, father of a multitude, and Sarai's name to Sarah, princess. God made a covenant with Abraham (Genesis 17:9–27) to establish the validity of His promise. Traditionally, a covenant is sealed by the two persons slashing their right palms and pressing their palms together to mix or mingle their blood. In this case, God told Abraham to circumcise himself, to cut off "the flesh of his foreskin," and the same should be done to all his male descendants. I believe there is a mistranslation here.

Since the foreskin is flesh, and the male organ, elsewhere, is also called flesh (see Ezekiel 16:26, 23:20, 44:7, 9 KJV), it should read "foreskin of the flesh" rather than "flesh of the foreskin." In both instances, the Hebrew word translated as *flesh* is the same.

There is a mystery here that had bothered me for years. Why did God choose circumcision as a sign of the covenant rather than some less traumatic and more obvious sign like a particular style of haircut or shape of the beard? Also what was God's part in the covenant? Was it merely to confirm the promise: "Do not be afraid, Abram. I am your shield, your exceedingly great reward," or something else? Also, for years I had wondered, if Jesus fulfilled all of the law and the prophets, how did He fulfill the law of circumcision?

In John 1:1–4, we read:

> In the beginning was the Word (Jesus), and the Word was with God, and the Word was God. He was in the beginning with God. All things were made through Him, and without Him nothing was made that was made. In Him was life, and the life was the light of men.

And the Word became flesh
and dwelt among us. (John 1:14)

Here we see Jesus, the creative Person of the Trinity, being sent to Earth by our loving heavenly Father to bring eternal light and life to lost humanity. He was rejected by mankind and was executed in the most horrible manner. The sinless Son of God died for the sins of the world. He shed His precious blood for mankind.

And after the sixty-two
weeks Messiah shall be cut off.
(Daniel 9:26)

He was taken from prison
and from judgment, and who
will declare His generation? For
He was cut off from the land of
the living; for the transgressions
of My people He was stricken.
(Isaiah 53:8)

Here we see Jesus, God in the flesh, the flesh of God, *yes, the Phallus of God,* being cut off. The creative organ of God. He shed His precious blood for the sins of the world. He did this willingly.

Looking unto Jesus, the
author and finisher of our faith,
who for the joy that was set before
Him endured the cross, despising

the shame, and has sat down at
the right hand of the throne of
God. (Hebrews 12:2)

This explains how Christ fulfilled the law of circumcision. God told Abraham to cut off the foreskin of his procreative organ, his phallus, *a prophetic act for all Jewish males to participate in.* God responded in an overwhelming manner *"circumcising" Himself by cutting off, amputating, the creative organ of the Godhead, His Phallus—a supreme act of love* (see Romans 8:3)!

What *love!* This act of God provided blood to wash away the sins of mankind, past, present, and future for all who will receive Jesus into their hearts. How can one not respond, unreservedly?

When Jesus arose from the dead, He appeared to the disciples in His glorified body.

Behold My hands and My
feet, that it is I Myself. Handle
Me and see, for a spirit does not
have flesh and bones as you see I
have. (Luke 24:39)

His body now consisted of flesh and bones. His precious blood had been sprinkled on the mercy seat of the heavenly Ark of the Covenant and shed abroad for the sins of mankind.

At the Last Supper, Jesus
took the cup of wine and said,

> "This cup is the new covenant
> in My blood, which is shed for
> you." (Luke 22:20)

At this point, it seems that the two terms *resurrection* and *erection* could be related. Again, don't be prudish. These are allegorical descriptions. The fact that Jesus described His resurrected body as flesh and bones would describe a sustained erection, which anyway is the definition of *phallus*. Let me hasten to explain. The seed of man in the Old Testament in the Hebrew language is defined as *sperm*, a term used by God many times in speaking to Abraham and others. Jesus, the flesh of God, said in the parable of the sower that the seed is the Word. It is understood that Jesus is the Sower of the seed (sperm). Jesus is also the baptizer of the Holy Ghost.[4]

> I indeed baptize you with
> water unto repentance. but he
> that cometh after me is might-
> ier than I, whose shoes I am not
> worthy to bear. He shall baptize
> you with the Holy Ghost, and
> with fire. (Spoken by John the
> Baptist in Matthew 3:11 KJV)

---

[4] *Holy Spirit* and *Holy Ghost* are synonymous referring to the Third Person of the Trinity.

Therefore, it follows that the semen of God is sperm, carried by the spermatic fluid, which has to be the Holy Spirit. When God pours out His Spirit, He is discharging seminal fluid into His people through His Phallus, Jesus. What *love*! [Joel 2:28; Acts 2:17; some will receive, others will not] Now we understand why Jesus said He must return to the Father so He could send the Holy Spirit, also returning for this reason:

> He that is wounded in the stones, or hath his privy member cut off, shall not enter into the congregation of the Lord. (Deuteronomy 23:1 KJV)

We have established that God does indeed have a phallus. Since there is a phallus, is there a female counterpart? Yes, of course!

While Adam was naming the animals, he could not help but see that every male had a mate. When he was finished with his assignment as mentioned before, I'm sure he confronted God about the fact that he was the only male without a mate. So God put him into a deep sleep and took a rib from the body of Adam and formed a woman, a bride for Adam. Her name is Bride of Adam.

The church today, the Body of Christ, is in a deep sleep. God is even now forming a bride for Jesus out of the Body of Christ. Her name is Bride of Christ.

If you visit a Pentecostal, Charismatic, or Full Gospel church that flows in the Spirit, you may be turned off by the loud music. Loud music is biblical:

Sing unto him a new song; play skillfully with a loud noise." (Psalm 33:3 KJV)

O clap your hands, all ye people; shout unto God with the voice of triumph. (Psalm 47:1 KJV)

But I will sing of thy power; yea, I will sing aloud of thy mercy in the morning: for thou hast been my defense and refuge in the day of my trouble. (Psalm 59:16 KJV)

Sing aloud unto God our strength: make a joyful noise unto the God of Jacob. (Psalm 81:1 KJV)

Make a joyful noise unto the Lord, all the earth: make a loud noise, and rejoice, and sing praise. (Psalm 98:4 KJV)

> Praise him upon the loud
> cymbals: praise him upon the
> high-sounding cymbals. (Psalm
> 150:5 KJV)

The definition of the Hebrew word translated *aloud* is "to shout for joy." Additionally, in Psalm 22:3 (KJV), David wrote, "But thou art holy, O Thou that inhabits the praises of Israel." Singing praises to God by the body of believers, especially in the sanctuary, brings the Holy Spirit onto the scene. He inhabits our praises. The intention of the Holy Spirit is to focus our attention on Jesus. Praise and worship songs magnify Jesus, singing praises to Him directly. Most traditional hymns, if they are about Jesus are often just that, about Him, not praising Him directly. Songs of praise addressing Jesus directly have a greater anointing or spiritual aura.

As you enter into praise and worship:

> Lift your hands in the sanc-
> tuary and bless the Lord. (Psalm
> 134:2 KJV)

> Thus will I bless thee while
> I live: I will lift up my hands in
> thy name. (Psalm 63:4 KJV)

> Hear the voice of my sup-
> plications, when I cry unto thee,

> when I lift up my hands toward
> thy holy oracle. (Psalm 28:2 KJV)

> Let them praise his name in
> the dance: let them sing praises
> unto him with the timbrel and
> harp. (Psalm 149:3 KJV)

> Praise him with the tim-
> brel and dance: praise him with
> stringed instruments and organs.
> (Psalm 150:4 KJV)

In praise and worship, you are making love with Jesus Himself. If you are spiritually sensitive, you can soon sense the presence of the Holy Spirit and gradually you can sense a climax coming. Often at the climax, prophecies, exhortations, or a message in tongues will come forth followed by the interpretation, which is thrilling to hear as it is God speaking through these persons, *expressing His love and encouragement to His people, verbally.* Then the pastor preaches, and that is the seed or sperm of God being scattered for teaching and edification. Intercourse, climax, implantation. As that seed is received into one's heart, it will take root as in the good soil in the parable of the sower and the result is fruit-bearing in your life: love, joy, peace, long-suffering, gentleness, goodness, faith, meekness, temperance (self-control) (Galatians 5:22–23).

This is true fertility. Then the fruit produces more seeds to be scattered to others, which builds the Kingdom! These attributes, fruits of the Spirit, do not develop by our own efforts. They develop in our life as we focus on Jesus, reading the Word, praying, giving thanks, praising, and worshiping Him.

When we understand these things about God, He is not as far away as we thought! And the "precious blood of Jesus" takes on new significance.

CHAPTER 5

Song of Solomon

AT THE TIME THAT KING Solomon wrote this song, he had sixty wives and eighty concubines. Eventually, there were seven hundred wives and three hundred concubines. His first wife was the daughter of Egypt's pharaoh. His other wives were the daughters of the other ruling monarchs, governors, and VIPs of the surrounding nations. I believe his concubines were Israeli women. He was also surrounded by many virgins vying with each other to become concubines so they, too, could live in the lap of luxury.

By marrying into the royal families of the nations, Solomon was able to establish trade with them and became fabulously wealthy. He undoubtedly greatly improved the economy of the Middle East, if not of the then-known world. Also throughout his forty-year reign, there was peace, unlike with his father King David. Read the story-song.

The story is a sensuous song that Solomon wrote about his favorite concubine whom he calls the Shulamite, a black woman from Shula. She was his most beloved because he wrote about her and apparently none other. She lived in the suburbs of Jerusalem and had a job working in the vineyards and possibly tending sheep. She had a boyfriend, a shepherd, with whom she had frequent trysts, which was okay with the king because he was unable to see her very often having the choice of very many women to sleep with every night. Concubines of that day and even today are frequent overnight gifts to visiting businessmen and heads of state, providing entertainment and intimacy.

One night, when the Shulamite was asleep, there was a knock on the door, which woke her up. It was her shepherd boyfriend. It was not a good time for lovemaking. It was not convenient. She had bathed the evening before and didn't want to get her feet dirty on the dirt floor of her shanty. She tried in the darkness to find her gown. When she eventually got to the door to open it, he was gone. Now finally, fully awake, she was sorry that she had missed him and ran out into the dark street (no streetlights in Jerusalem back then) calling for her lover. The watchmen of the city (two or more) found her, attacked her, pulled off her gown (translated as veil), and undoubtedly raped her.

I agree that this is a picture of Christ and the church. But it is the story of two lovers and two loved ones. King Solomon is a type of Jesus, of course. The boyfriend is a type of the world. The loved ones are two groups in the church. The one group is asleep and finds their relationship with Jesus to frequently be inconvenient. They have a ho-hum attitude in their relationship with Him. Frequently, their lives are fraught with difficulties since they are living outside of the umbrella of the Lord's protection and blessing.

The other group is deeply in love with their Lord, engaging in the most intimate lovemaking you can imagine. Their lovemaking takes place in the King's bedchamber. The Shulamite even describes the King's bed. It is designed like a chariot.

The Song of Solomon is a depiction of the church of today before the Bride has been drawn out.

In several places in the New Testament, the unity (oneness) of the church is called for or emphasized. In Jesus's prayer to the Father in John 17, He is praying for oneness not only with and among His disciples but also among all of His followers including, I'm sure, the five hundred brethren that He revealed Himself to at one time following His resurrection (1 Corinthians 15:6). In the books of Romans and 1 Corinthians, we read:

> For as we have many members in one body, but all the members do not have the same function, so we, being many, are one body in Christ, and individually members of one another. (Romans 12:4–5)

> For by one Spirit we were all
> baptized into one body—whether
> Jews or Greeks, whether slaves or
> free—and have all been made to
> drink into one Spirit. For in fact
> the body is not one member but
> many. (1 Corinthians 12:13–14)

Paul emphasizes that the Body of Christ is one with many members. The fact that there are two groups in the church does not imply that there may not be oneness there. Jesus had many followers, but among these were twelve who were closer to Him. Among the twelve were three who were even closer. And then there was one whom Jesus loved. So it follows that the relationship of Jesus, the church, and the Bride will be like that.

CHAPTER 6

The Upper Room

Dr. Luke, in Acts chapter 1, wrote the following:

> The former account I made, O Theophilus, of all that Jesus began both to do and teach, until the day in which He was taken up, after He through the Holy Spirit had given commandments to the apostles whom He had chosen, to whom He also presented Himself alive after His suffering by many infallible proofs, being seen by them during forty days and speaking of the things pertaining to the kingdom of God.
>
> And being assembled together with them, He commanded them not to depart from

Jerusalem, but to wait for the Promise of the Father, "which," He said, "you have heard from Me; for John truly baptized with water, but you shall be baptized with the Holy Spirit not many days from now." Therefore, when they had come together, they asked Him, saying, "Lord, will You at this time restore the kingdom to Israel?" And He said to them, "It is not for you to know times or seasons which the Father has put in His own authority. But you shall receive power when the Holy Spirit has come upon you; and you shall be witnesses to Me in Jerusalem, and in all Judea and Samaria, and to the end of the earth."

Now when He had spoken these things, while they watched, He was taken up, and a cloud received Him out of their sight. (Acts 1:1–9)

Jesus had appeared in those forty days following His resurrection not only to the disciples or apostles but also to many others of his followers including those five hundred brethren. I'm sure the word got around to all of them that Jesus had commanded that they were to wait in Jerusalem for the manifestation of God's promise to be baptized in the Holy Ghost to receive power to be witnesses unto Him for the whole world. On the day of Pentecost, there were 120 present in an Upper Room (Acts 1:13).

> When the Day of Pentecost had fully come, they were all with one accord in one place. And suddenly there came a sound from heaven, as of a rushing mighty wind, and it filled the whole house where they were sitting. Then there appeared to them divided tongues, as of fire, and one sat upon each of them. And they were all filled with the Holy Spirit and began to speak with other tongues, as the Spirit gave them utterance.

> And there were dwelling in Jerusalem Jews, devout men, from every nation under heaven. And when this sound occurred, the multitude came together, and were confused, because everyone heard them speak in his own language. Then they were all amazed and marveled, saying to

one another, "Look, are not all these who speak Galileans? And how is it that we hear, each in our own language in which we were born?" (Acts 2:1–8)

Instead of the apostles having to leave on short notice "to the end of the earth," God had representatives from "every nation under heaven" already present, a captive audience. Peter stood up and preached his first sermon, impromptu, and three thousand souls were saved and baptized! This was how the church was founded, in the mighty power of the Holy Ghost! Later, other gifts of the Holy Spirit manifested. These are the following: word of wisdom, word of knowledge, faith, gifts of healing, working of miracles, prophecy, discerning of spirits, different kinds of tongues, interpretation of tongues (1 Corinthians 12:8–10).

Jesus here, through His apostles, was establishing His church in the Earth. These gifts when in operation have a mighty impact in building the church, again regrettably, not so much in America as in Third-World countries. The church in America has long since decided that this was just for the *early church* and not for the *church of today*. *Early church* and *church of today* are misnomers. The church is the church regardless of time frame. Jesus intended for His saints to receive the baptism of the Holy Ghost and His gifts to build His church into a mighty army for the Kingdom of God, for the pulling down of satanic strongholds worldwide, and for the salvation of multitudes of souls. Denial of the baptism of the Holy Spirit, His gifts, power, and boldness is the reason that the church in the Western world is so powerless and so vulnerable to the works of the devil! *This is why the church is not the Bride!* Members of the Bride are those deeply in love with Jesus, have received the Holy Spirit in His fullness, and operate in one or more gifts of the Spirit. The Bride is those who continue in His Word with prayer, fasting, giving thanks, praising Jesus, and evangelizing. As Rebekah received Eliezer's gifts, so should the church be receiving and operating in the gifts of the Holy Spirit.

Many would say, "Well, I just want to get inside Heaven, and I'll be satisfied. I'll just do what it takes to get inside the gates." If your intention is to just squeak through the gates, you run a big risk of not getting in at all. 1 Peter 4:18 (KJV) says,

> If the righteous scarcely be saved, where shall the ungodly and sinner appear?

There will be various levels in Heaven[5], but the members of the Bride have the most intense relationship with Jesus with "joy unspeakable and full of Glory!"

---

[5] Based on 1 Corinthians 3:11–15, "gold, silver, precious stones, wood, hay, stubble," with the Bride, equaling seven levels.

On the day of Pentecost, those 120 believers were in the Upper Room in Old Jerusalem when they were all filled with the Holy Ghost. There were 380 others who were apparently commanded to be there but did not go. They had to be close followers of Jesus, or He would not have revealed Himself to them following His resurrection. They are called *brethren*. Here we see the beginnings of the church where a majority apparently had other things to do. It was not convenient. Those who went and received, what would you call them? Pentecostals? "Well, yes," you'd say "But, but…" But what?

Selah, stop and think about this.

Momentarily, on the day of Pentecost, the church was the Bride; but immediately, the Bride was in the minority.

These two parables of Jesus, the sower, and the ten virgins, seem to be closely related. Let us review the parable of the sower in chapter 3. This same parable is also recorded in Matthew 13 and Luke 8 with slight differences.

In the case of the first soil, the person characterized by the wayside who receives the Word in his heart does not understand it or does not believe it; the soil, his heart, was not prepared. The Word is snatched by the devil "lest they believe and be saved." This person is a lost soul.

In the case of the stony ground, this person receives the Word gladly, with joy, and believes for a while, but because there is no root or because of tribulation, persecution, or temptation, he becomes offended and falls away. The definition of *offended* is "departing, leaving, withdrawing or falling away from the faith." This person, too, may be a lost soul. But with repentance can be restored.

In the case of the soil with the thorns, this person hears and receives the Word, but because of the cares of this world, deceitfulness of riches, and lusts of other things including pleasures, the Word is choked, and this Christian is unfruitful. This describes much of the church today. It is the Bride that is good ground, is honest with a good heart, hears, understands, keeps the Word, and bears fruit with patience (Luke 8:15).

One has to examine oneself to determine which category one is in. If you are a believer, and you continue to believe in Jesus, then you have been sealed by the Spirit of God as the Apostle Paul has written:

> In Him (Christ) you also trusted, after you heard the word of truth, the gospel of your salvation; in whom also, having believed, you were sealed with the Holy Spirit of promise. (Ephesians 1:13)

> And do not grieve the Holy Spirit of God, by whom you were sealed for the day of redemption. (Ephesians 4:30)

Now He who establishes us with you in Christ and has anointed us is God, who also has sealed us and given us the Spirit in our hearts as a guarantee. (2 Corinthians 1:21–22)

Also, in Romans 8:38–39, Paul wrote:

For I am persuaded that neither death nor life, nor angels nor principalities nor powers, nor things present nor things to come, nor height nor depth, nor any other created thing, shall be able to separate us from the love of God which is in Christ Jesus our Lord.

By these Scriptures, we have the assurance of salvation. The whole epistle of 1 John is written that we can have assurance of salvation (1 John 5:13). At the same time, we need to know that our attitude toward Jesus, now, will be reflected back to us in the hereafter as in Mark 8:38 and Luke 9:26:

For whoever is ashamed of Me and My words, of him the Son of Man will be ashamed when He comes in His own

glory, and in His Father's, and of
the holy angels.

Jesus, in His Sermon on the Mount, exhorts the multitude:

> Therefore you shall be per-
> fect, just as your Father in heaven
> is perfect. (Matthew 5:48)

The Apostle Paul also wrote in 2 Corinthians 13:11:

> Finally, brethren, farewell.
> Become complete ("Be perfect"
> in KJV). Be of good comfort, be
> of one mind, live in peace; and
> the God of love and peace will be
> with you.

Now we know we cannot attain true perfection in this life, nor can we earn salvation by trying to be perfect. Perfection comes to saved ones when we are resurrected or raptured. That's when corruption and mortality are replaced with incorruption and immortality (1 Corinthians 15:50–54), and Christ will have cleansed the church by washing her[6] with the water of the Word, to "present her to Himself a glorious

---

[6] Personal pronouns in ancient Greek are interchangeable. In KJV, the church is referred to as *it*.

church, not having spot or wrinkle or any such thing, but that she should be holy and without blemish" (Ephesians 5:25–27). He gives her a spiritual bath, before the wedding, resulting in spiritual virginity or innocence. (This is speaking of the church, not only the Bride.) We cannot do this for ourselves. Jesus does this, like when He gives us the free gift of salvation.

Most folks believe this passage of scripture, Ephesians 5:23–27, speaks of the church being the Bride:

> For the husband is head of the wife, as also Christ is head of the church; and He is the Savior of the body. Therefore, just as the church is subject to Christ, so let the wives be to their own husbands in everything.

> Husbands, love your wives, just as Christ also loved the church and gave Himself for her, that He might sanctify and cleanse her with the washing of water by the word, that He might present her to Himself a glorious church, not having spot or wrinkle or any such thing, but that she should be holy and without blemish.

Church, here, is not the Bride. Verse 23 confirms that the church is the Body of Christ. To clarify, even as Peter, James, and John would be considered as the *elite* for lack of a better term among the disciples of Christ, so would the Bride be considered as the elite of the church!

Upper Room is mentioned three times in the New Testament, twice in the Gospels where the Last Supper was held, and once in the book of Acts, where the 120 folks were gathered in Old Jerusalem on the Day of Pentecost. I believe the parable of the ten virgins has to do with entering the Upper Room in the Holy City, New Jerusalem, which would be the Bridal Chamber.

> Then the kingdom of heaven shall be likened to ten virgins who took their lamps and went out to meet the bridegroom. Now five of them were wise, and five were foolish. Those who were foolish took their lamps and took no oil with them, but the wise took oil in their vessels with their lamps. But while the bridegroom was delayed, they all slumbered and slept.
>
> And at midnight a cry was heard: "Behold, the bridegroom is coming; go out to meet him!"

Then all those virgins arose and trimmed their lamps. And the foolish said to the wise, "Give us some of your oil, for our lamps are going out." But the wise answered, saying, "No, lest there should not be enough for us and you; but go rather to those who sell, and buy for yourselves." And while they went to buy, the bridegroom came, and those who were ready went in with him to the wedding; and the door was shut.

Afterward the other virgins came also, saying, "Lord, Lord, open to us!" But he answered and said, "Assuredly, I say to you, I do not know you." [see Genesis 24:16; 1 Kings 1:4; Matthew 1:24–25]

Watch therefore, for you know neither the day nor the hour in which the *Son of Man is coming*. (Matthew 25:1–13).

Oil, here, is indicative of the Holy Spirit. The foolish virgins had brought oil in their lamps but none in vessels. The wise virgins brought oil in their lamps but more in their vessels. The foolish virgins had been born again. They had been raptured. They had received a measure of the Spirit when they had gotten saved. They did what was required to get through the gates. They had gotten their membership card but had not made any investment into this *sure-thing, can't-lose* corporation. They had believed in Him and received His love but had not reciprocated in like manner. Spiritually, they are babies, toddlers, adolescents, tweens, and not ready for marriage. So the Bridegroom told them He didn't know them *intimately*. It was not the same rejection as in Luke 13:27, where it says:

> I tell you I do not know you,
> where you are from. Depart from
> Me, all you workers of iniquity.

These foolish virgins had been taught that the church is the Bride of Christ, but they had rejected the Upper Room experience in Old Jerusalem, so now they were turned away at the door of the Upper Room, the Bridal Chamber in New Jerusalem by the Bridegroom Himself, Jesus. "Many are called but few are chosen," resonates here (Matthew 20:16).

To put it simply, the difference between the wise and foolish virgins is this: When the foolish virgins received salvation, the portion of the Holy Spirit, which was imparted to them, was *sealing* by the Spirit, providing guaranteed possession for redemption (see John 20:22). Whereas, in addition, the wise virgins prayed to receive the baptism of the Holy

Spirit, which resulted in the *filling* of their vessels, their whole being becoming infused with the Holy Spirit!

At Pentecost, the believers prayed for ten days before they received. Since then, the baptism is received much more quickly. However, *one needs to pray and ask for this experience in order to receive it* (see Luke 11:13).

The parable of the ten virgins can be illustrated by the story of Mary, Martha, and Jesus (Luke 10:38–42). Martha invited Jesus into their home. Martha was distracted by ADLs (activities of daily living). Mary sat down at the feet of Jesus and absorbed every word spoken by Him. This is Mary who also later anointed His feet with the expensive oil of spikenard and wiped them with her hair (John 12:3). It all boils down to the *intensity* of our love for our Lord and our obedience in following through.

If you haven't seen or communicated with a particular friend for a long time, your relationship suffers. So it is in the spirit realm with Jesus. Your relationship with Jesus should be like with your spouse—to be cherished, responded to, and never taken for granted.

When Jesus rebuked the disciples for chasing away the children,

> He said, "Let the little children come to Me, and do not forbid them; for of such is the kingdom of heaven." (Matthew 19:14)

In effect saying, "As a child clings to his parent, in like manner should you cling to your Father in Heaven!" (see Deuteronomy 30:20).

It appears that the five foolish virgins represent very many in the church. If the church is not the Bride, then what role is played by the church? Obviously, the selection of the Bride takes place before the marriage. John the Baptist in John 3:29 indicated that he will be the best man at the wedding. Of course, every wedding has guests. So, surely, the guests will be the saints of the church, in addition to the angels.

> And the Spirit and the bride say, "Come!" And let him who hears say, "Come!" And let him who thirsts come. Whoever desires, let him take the water of life freely. (Revelation 22:17)

Everyone partakes of the marriage supper of the Lamb, and what a feast that will be! So after the wedding, what will be the role of the church? In the Song of Solomon, since King Solomon represents King Jesus, he had many wives and also many concubines, and the Bride is made up of many members who are now wives of Jesus. Guess who the concubines must be?

Historically, in many kingdoms, the concubines were involved with administrative duties, ruling and reigning? I believe the Bride has a very special and different relationship with Jesus. According to the writer of Hebrews, there is a level of spiritual life yet to be attained.

> Therefore, leaving the discussion of the elementary principles of Christ, let us go on to perfection, not laying again the foundation of repentance from dead works and of faith toward God, of the doctrine of baptisms, of laying on of hands, of resurrection of the dead, and of eternal judgment. And this we will do if God permits. (Hebrews 6:1–3)

Allegorically, while the philosophers, theologians, Bible scholars, and church leaders are downstairs sitting around the table discussing, disputing, and arguing concerning issues, doctrine, differences of opinion, and interpretation that are divisive and schismatic, the Bride is upstairs in bed with Jesus!

Can you not see that, when you receive salvation, you actually become engaged to Jesus? Then, as a fiancé or fiancée of Jesus, the process of sanctification would be your courtship with Him before the marriage.

Even as many fiancés and fiancées resist making the final decision to marry, so also do believers resist receiving the baptism of the Holy Spirit. Making the transition from fiancé or fiancée (concubine) to spouse[7] requires overcoming that resistance and praying for the marriage to take place.

Your marriage to Jesus will take place when you receive the baptism of the Holy Spirit. The offspring of this union would be new souls being born (again) into the Kingdom. The wedding and marriage feast in Heaven will formalize and celebrate what has already taken place on earth between you and Jesus!

Receiving this baptism opens up a whole new dimension of Christian living, making possible a much closer walk with the Lord. This experience will differ from one person to another. For myself, I received a new conscience; a breaking of demonic stronghold (addiction); a deeper understanding of the Word; a greater love for others; an increased ability to resist temptation; an authority and power over demonic activity; and a new avenue of communication with God—praying in the spirit (in tongues).

It is by the Holy Spirit that our marriage with Jesus is consummated. As a wife is the receptacle of her husband's fountain of love, *so also are we the receptacles of God's fountain of love who is the Holy Spirit through Jesus!*

---

[7] Even as the church is made up of males and females, so also is the Bride.

CHAPTER 7

New Jerusalem

In Revelation 21:1–2, the Apostle John writes:

> Now I saw a new heaven
> and a new earth, for the first
> heaven and the first earth had
> passed away. Also there was no
> more sea. Then I, John, saw the
> holy city, New Jerusalem, coming
> down out of heaven from God,
> prepared as a bride adorned for
> her husband.

John says here that he saw a New Heaven[8] and a New Earth and then states that he also saw the Holy City, New Jerusalem, descending from God out of Heaven. Many Bible scholars say that the New

---

[8] *New heaven* here is not the universe but the first heaven, which is the atmosphere around our planet.

Heaven and New Earth's re-creation takes place at the end of the age, that is, after the one-thousand-year reign of Christ on the Earth. Some also say that the arrival of New Jerusalem will be at that same time.

I believe otherwise: After the nuclear war with its radiation, extensive destruction on Earth with all the toxic waste, bloody seas and rivers, rubble on the ground, and the junk in space, also in the aftermath of the Great Tribulation that Jesus would want to clean it all up at the beginning of His millennial reign. Therefore, the New Heaven and the New Earth's re-creation could very well take place immediately after the Battle of Armageddon.

Undoubtedly, this is when Isaiah 40:1–5 will be fulfilled!

> "Comfort, yes, comfort My people!"
> Says your God.
> "Speak comfort to Jerusalem, and cry out to her,
> That her warfare is ended,
> That her iniquity is pardoned;
> For she has received from the Lord's hand.
> Double for all her sins."
> The voice of one crying in the wilderness:
> "Prepare the way of the Lord;

> Make straight in the desert.
> A highway for our God.
> Every valley shall be exalted.
> And every mountain and
> hill brought low;
> The crooked places shall be
> made straight.
> And the rough places
> smooth;
> The glory of the Lord shall
> be revealed,
> And all flesh shall see *it*
> together;
> For the mouth of the Lord
> has spoken."

Also, it says there will be no more sea. With the oceans gone, there would be an extreme change in weather patterns. Perhaps there will be a return to the days of the Garden of Eden when the Earth was watered by underground streams with a mist rising from the earth (Genesis 2:6). God's sprinkler system.

In Revelation 21:9–11, John writes that one of God's angels told him, "Come, I will show you the Bride, the Lamb's Wife." John was carried away "in the spirit" to a "great and high mountain," perhaps the moon, and was shown "the great city, the Holy Jerusalem descending out of Heaven from God." It looked like one huge jewel of many colors, "having the Glory of God." The city is of pure transparent gold with walls of jasper.

Jasper can be found in many different colors: red, green, brown, orange, blue, or yellow. The city glowed with its own interior light source, God Himself. No wonder John describes its beauty "as a bride adorned for her husband." It was the glory of God!

Can you imagine the enormity of this city? John describes it as being 1,500 miles (about 2,400 km) square at the base and 1,500 miles (about 2,400 km) high. If it was sitting on the Earth, it would extend into the stratosphere six times higher than the 248-mile-high orbit of the International Space Station. The area at the base being 2,500,000 square miles (nearly twice the area of India) would cover 72 percent of the contiguous forty-eight states of the US or 20 percent of the surface of Africa. The wall of this enormous structure is 216 feet thick. It has twelve foundations garnished with twelve different kinds of precious stones, the foundations named for the twelve apostles of Christ. There are twelve gates of pearl, each named for one of the twelve tribes of Israel. The gates will be open 24-7 with an angel guarding each gate. With the circumference at the base of the city being six thousand miles, the gates will average five hundred miles apart.

If New Jerusalem would be located over the Middle East and centered over Old Jerusalem, its base would cover all of Egypt, the eastern one-fourth of the Mediterranean Sea, most of Greece, and all of Turkey, Syria, Bulgaria, and Georgia; the southern half of the Black Sea; the western one-fourth of Iran, all of Iraq and Jordan, and most of Saudi Arabia; the northern one-third of Sudan; and the eastern one-third of Libya. To preserve these populations, it stands to reason that there has to be a re-creation of the Earth. The seas must go to make room or space for the land masses and nations to be shifted out from the Middle East. In 1 Chronicles 1:19, we read,

> In the days of Peleg the Earth was divided.

This was many years after the flood of Noah. Isaiah prophesied in Isaiah 40:4,

> Every valley shall be exalted and every mountain and hill brought low.

Undoubtedly, to be fulfilled at the creation of a New Heaven and a New Earth, Mount Ararat will be flattened, and the ice will melt exposing Noah's Ark for the world to see! When this is done and new roads and bridges are built, Earth people will then be able to drive 24,900 miles around the globe in their cars!

Since the Earth was created from water (Genesis 1:9), it would be reasonable to assume that re-creation of the Earth could very well be that God turns the oceans into dry land, creating perhaps, a huge new Garden of Eden! This could very well be done without disturbing the populations of the nations!

The main benefit for mankind with the removal of the seas will be the resulting ease of access of the nations of the world to New Jerusalem. When John, the revelator, saw in the spirit the New Jerusalem's descent, he wrote,

> And I heard a loud voice from heaven saying, "Behold, the tabernacle of God is with men, and He will dwell with them, and they shall be His people. God Himself will be with them and be their God." (Revelation 21:3)

When this happens, it is commanded that all peoples of the earth are to come and worship at the annual Feast of Tabernacles.

> And it shall come to pass that everyone who is left of all the nations which came against Jerusalem shall go up from year to year to worship the King, the Lord of hosts, and to keep the Feast of Tabernacles. And it shall be that whichever of the families of the earth do not come up to Jerusalem to worship the King, the Lord of hosts, on them there will be no rain. If the fam-

ily[9] of Egypt will not come up and enter in, they shall have no rain; they shall receive the plague with which the Lord strikes the nations who do not come up to keep the Feast of Tabernacles.

This shall be the punishment of Egypt and the punishment of all the nations that do not come up to keep the Feast of Tabernacles. (Zechariah 14:16–19)

With the throne of God and Jesus being in New Jerusalem, the City of God will quickly become the center of worship, government, and the capital of the world. Superhighways will be built from all corners of the earth converging on New Jerusalem. With the seas gone, there will be little excuse for anyone to not make a pilgrimage to the Holy Land to worship our Lord and Savior, Jesus Christ, *in person!*

There is some controversy as to whether the city is shaped like a cube or a pyramid. Based on a number of scriptures, it is most certainly in the shape of a pyramid. There are seven scriptures in the New Testament and one in the Old Testament that refer to "the stone which the builders rejected has become the head of the corner."

---

[9] family – singular – could mean a family member or representative(s) of the nation?

The stone which the builders rejected has become the chief cornerstone. (Psalm 118:22)

Jesus said to them, "Have you never read in the Scriptures: 'The stone which the builders rejected.

Has become the chief cornerstone. This was the Lord's doing,

And it is marvelous in our eyes'"? (Matthew 21:42)

Have you not even read this Scripture:

"The stone which the builders rejected Has become the chief cornerstone." (Mark 12:10)

Then He looked at them and said, "What then is this that is written: 'The stone which the builders rejected.

Has become the chief cornerstone'?" (Luke 20:17)

This is the "stone which was rejected by you builders, which has become the chief cornerstone." (Acts 4:11)

[H]aving been built on the foundation of the apostles and prophets, Jesus Christ Himself being the chief cornerstone, in whom the whole building, being fitted together, grows into a holy temple in the Lord, in whom you also are being built together for a dwelling place of God in the Spirit. (Ephesians 2:20–22)

Therefore it is also contained in the Scripture, "Behold, I lay in Zion.

A chief cornerstone, elect, precious,

And he who believes on Him will by no means be put to shame." (1 Peter 2:6)

Therefore, to you who believe, He is precious; but to those who are disobedient,

"The stone which the builders rejected Has become the chief cornerstone." (1 Peter 2:7)

The builders of the city were angels; I believe they had been building on the city for thousands of years. They rejected that stone because of its shape. They knew that there was only one spot in the whole structure where it would fit, at the very apex, where the four corners converge. It is the capstone, which was put in place, no doubt, when Jesus on the cross declared, "It is finished" (John 19:30)! Jesus is that Cornerstone (Ephesians 2:20).

New Jerusalem has many names: the Bride, Mount Zion, Mountain of God, High and Holy Place, House of God, Tabernacle of God, Habitation of God, and High Tower. God and Jesus will have their throne there.

> And there shall be no more
> curse: but the throne of God
> and of the Lamb shall be in it:
> and his servants shall serve Him.
> (Revelation 22:3)

Another mystery that I have wondered about for years: When Jesus's feet touch the Mount of Olives on His return to Earth, why will the Mount of Olives be split East to West and create a "very great valley"? (KJV).

> And in that day His feet will
> stand on the Mount of Olives,
> Which faces Jerusalem on the
> east.
> And the Mount of Olives
> shall be split in two, From east to
> west,
> Making a very large valley;

> Half of the mountain shall
> move toward the north And half
> of it toward the south (Zachariah
> 14:4)

Here is the probable answer: to create a landing site for New Jerusalem! Will Old Jerusalem be crushed? No, of course not. It is, and has been, the City of God for thousands of years. New Jerusalem will settle down gently over Old Jerusalem with her people. Israel and all of the land God promised Abraham will be absorbed completely intact to be part of the ground level of the New City of God. Here are two corroborating scriptures that read the same, I'm sure for emphasis: Isaiah 2:2–3 and Micah 4:1–2:

Isaiah:

> Now it shall come to pass in
> the latter days That the mountain
> of the Lord's house.
> Shall be established on the
> top of the mountains, And shall
> be exalted above the hills;
> And all nations shall flow to
> it. Many people shall come and
> say,
> "Come, and let us go up to
> the mountain of the Lord, To the
> house of the God of Jacob;
> He will teach us His ways,

And we shall walk in His paths."
For out of Zion shall go forth the law,
And the word of the Lord from Jerusalem.

Micah:

Now it shall come to pass in the latter days That the mountain of the Lord's house.
Shall be established on the top of the mountains, And shall be exalted above the hills;
And peoples shall flow to it. Many nations shall come and say,
"Come, and let us go up to the mountain of the Lord, To the house of the God of Jacob;
He will teach us His ways,
And we shall walk in His paths."
For out of Zion the law shall go forth,
And the word of the Lord from Jerusalem.

Two other Scriptures seem to resonate here, that read the same: Matthew 23:37 and Luke 13:34:

> O Jerusalem, Jerusalem, the one who kills the prophets and stones those who are sent to her! How often I wanted to gather your children together, as a hen gathers her chicks under her wings, but you were not willing!

I believe that New Jerusalem will have three main levels:

Upper Level:

- The throne room of God and Jesus
- The Upper Room or Bridal Chamber
- Arena for the Bride of Christ
- Rooms for the Bride

Middle Level:

- Arena for the Body of Christ
- Rooms for the Saints of the Church

Ground Level:

- The nation of Israel, including all the land that God promised Abraham
- Arena for Israel, Wife of God
- Rooms for the Israelites, the Jews

If you were looking for or expecting a mansion in the city of New Jerusalem, you may instead find it on Planet Heaven, which I have been told is a million miles in diameter. That's where you will find most of the angels, horse farms, your pets, and of course mansions!

After the one-thousand-year reign of Christ on Earth, there is an interpretation of Ephesians 1:10 that when all things in Heaven and Earth are gathered together in one, Planet Earth and Planet Heaven will be merged as one planet for eternity! *Hallelujah*!

CONCLUSION

IN THIS SMALL BOOK, I have sought to point out what I believe to be erroneous teaching in the church today concerning the Bride of Christ. I trust that I have been rightly dividing the Word. At the same time, I desire to challenge us all to a closer walk with our Lord Jesus. It behooves us all to wake up from our smug complacency and become more involved in the work of the ministry for the Kingdom of God!

If you are not a born-again Christian, you need to know that there is no other way to Heaven but through Jesus.

> "Most assuredly, I say to you, he who does not enter the sheepfold by the door, but climbs up some other way, the same is a thief and a robber. But he who enters by the door is the shepherd of the sheep. To him the door-keeper opens, and the sheep hear his voice; and he calls his own

sheep by name and leads them out.

And when he brings out his own sheep, he goes before them; and the sheep follow him, for they know his voice. Yet they will by no means follow a stranger, but will flee from him, for they do not know the voice of strangers." Jesus used this illustration, but they did not understand the things which He spoke to them.

Then Jesus said to them again, "Most assuredly, I say to you, I am the door of the sheep. All who ever came before Me are thieves and robbers, but the sheep did not hear them. I am the door. If anyone enters by Me, he will be saved, and will go in and out and find pasture. The thief does not come except to steal, and to kill, and to destroy. I have come that they may have life, and that they may have it more abundantly.

"I am the good shepherd. The good shepherd gives His life for the sheep. But a hireling, he who is not the shepherd, one who does not own the sheep, sees the wolf coming and leaves the sheep and flees; and the wolf catches the sheep and scatters them. The hireling flees because he is a hireling and does not care about the sheep. I am the good shepherd; and I know My sheep, and am known by My own. As the Father knows Me, even so I know the Father; and I lay down My life for the sheep." (John 10:1–15).

Jesus said to him (Thomas), "I am the way, the truth, and the life. No one comes to the Father except through Me." (John 14:6)

The Holy Bible is our only source on Earth that truthfully and comprehensively tells us the origin of the universe, the origin of life, and how we came to be, and above all, that there is God behind it all. Don't you think it the height of folly and stupidity, or the depth thereof, to go anywhere else to find your way to Heaven, when the answer is as plain as the nose on your face? This is the same book, the only book in existence, that informs you that there is such a place called Heaven! So why would you not follow the plan put forth therein, the instructions on how to get there? You can't get there by your own effort. No religion on Earth can help you get there. Christianity is not a religion. It is a relationship with Jesus Christ. Religions are man-made, *counterfeit*.

Jesus has redeemed you and bought you back from Satan. He has bought and paid for your ticket to Heaven, a free pass, a *free gift* of salvation! To receive this *free gift*, you must admit that you are a sinner, give up your attempts to *find* yourself and *find out* who you really are or who you are supposed to be, which in God's eyes is rebellion. Living your life by doing it "my way" is a defiant rebellion against God. You need to submit yourself and your waywardness and invite Him into your heart and life to become your Savior and Lord. Allow Him to be on the throne of your life, kicking yourself off! Then He will direct your path through life. He will show you who you are—His precious child.

Many people looking forward to their retirement years are trusting in their 401K, IRA, or income from investments. Not many give much thought to their future after death.

Retirement years last ten, twenty, or maybe even thirty years, which is but a drop in the ocean compared to eternity. Eternity goes on and on forever. Wise folks put their trust in Jesus, living their lives to honor and glorify Him. Foolish folks who reject Jesus are choosing hell as their destination. How long do you think it would take burning in those flames before you regret rejecting God's love and His *free gift* of salvation? Surely before the first billion years of you screaming at the top of your lungs! Denying that hell exists will not make it go away. *Hell was not designed for mankind but for the devil and the fallen angels. You can choose not to go there!*

Pray this simple prayer:

Lord Jesus, I repent of my sins. Come into my heart. I make You my Lord and Savior.

If you mean this from the bottom of your heart, according to the Word of God, you are *born again*. *And by your choice to accept God's free gift of salvation, you have just changed your eternal destination!*

You need to follow up this decision by developing a personal relationship with Jesus. You do this with Bible reading, praying, giving thanks, praising, and worshiping Him. To help with this, you need to join yourself in a Bible-believing, teaching, preaching church, ideally a Full Gospel, Pentecostal, or Charismatic church,[10] where you can also receive the baptism of the Holy Spirit and become a part of the Bride of Christ!

---

[10] Assembly of God and Church of God are also Pentecostal churches, along with numerous nondenominational churches.

ABOUT THE AUTHOR

As the son of a Mennonite professor and pastor, John Gehman has been a lifelong student of the Bible. He also practiced medicine as a general practitioner until his retirement in 2022 at the age of eighty-six. The last sixteen years of practice were dedicated to serving the elderly and disabled in their homes. After his retirement, he decided to put his years of biblical study and free time to good use by writing this book. He and his wife, Joy Namwanje, have been married for eleven years and live in a small, rural town in south-central Virginia. With the help of his daughter and her daughters, they opened a Christian elementary school in Kampala, Uganda, Joy's hometown. They are members of Faith Landmarks Ministries in Richmond, Virginia.